P9-CAM-281

Résumé Rescue!

Résumé Rescue!

A How-To Manual
by
Stephen Summerford

E & E Publishing
Sausalito, California

WEST BEND LIBRARY

Résumé Rescue!
A How-To Manual
Copyright © 2004 Stephen Summerford
ISBN 0-9748933-0-7

All rights reserved. This book may not be reproduced in
whole or in part in any form, or by any means, without
written permission from the publisher.

Published by
E & E Publishing
1001 Bridgeway, # 227
Sausalito, California 94965
U.S.A.
Website: www.EandEGroup.com/Publishing
Email: EandEGroup@EandEGroup.com

Originally issued in Ebook format by E & E Publishing
Copyright © 2002   ISBN 0-9719898-4-2

Publisher's Cataloging-in-Publication Data
(Prepared by The Donohue Group, Inc.)

Summerford, Stephen.
    Résumé rescue! : a how-to manual / by Stephen
    Summerford.
        p. cm.
    Originally issued in Ebook format by E & E Publishing,
    c2002.
        ISBN: 0-9748933-0-7
1. Resumes (Employment)--Handbooks, manuals, etc. 2.
Job hunting. I. Title.

HF5383 .S86 2004
650.14'2—-dc21

Printed in U.S.A.

650.14
sub

Dedication
For my loving wife, Melissa,
without whom this manual would not be
possible.

Table of Contents

Introduction

You're looking for a job and you need help with your résumé *fast*.

There are plenty of résumé books on the market that go on—and on—for hundreds of pages. But if you need a job *now*, you probably don't have time to wade through all that ink and pick out the important points.

That's why I've written this little book: to give you the *meat* of résumé writing—without all the baloney. This manual tells you step-by-step how to write a professional résumé. Follow the instructions and your résumé will be a winner!

Whether you're a rocket scientist or a high school dropout, *Résumé Rescue!* will help you get the job that's right for you.

How to Write a Résumé

These are the steps to follow when writing a résumé:

1. Set your sights. Ask yourself what kind of job you are applying for.

2. Review your background. List on scratch paper all the things in your background that show why you would be good for the job.

3. Organize your notes. Put at the top of your résumé the information most relevant to the job you are applying for.

4. Edit your notes. Use the key words and phrases that tell an employer you are an active and responsible employee.

5. Type your résumé. Lay out the text neatly and in such a way that the important information stands out.

6. Write a cover letter to send with your résumé.

I will show you how to do each step.

Step 1 — Set Your Sights

Ask yourself what kind of job you are applying for. Write it down. Be specific. For example:

Job Objective: Senior Technical Writer for software company

Job Objective: President of airline company

Job Objective: Plumber in mid-sized company

Job Objective: Loan Officer at bank

Job Objective: Telemarketer

Job Objective: Executive Secretary in insurance company

Job Objective: Entry-level job in retail store

Job Objective: Marketing Director of publishing house

Keep your Job Objective in front of you while you do Step 2.

Step 2 — Review Your Background

List on scratch paper all the things in your background that show why you would be good for the job. Emphasize the positive but don't lie.

Use the categories below to guide you. I will go over each one. Depending on your background and experience, you'll have more things to list for some categories than for others.

Work Experience
Volunteer Experience
Life Experience
Personal Qualities
Education
Interests/Hobbies
Languages
Awards/Honors

If possible, ask a friend or family member to help you. Have them remind you of your good points and good things you've done. Family and friends often know us better than we know ourselves!

Step 2.1 – Work Experience

"Work Experience" is work for which you get paid.

Write this heading at the top of a sheet of scratch paper. Then list your jobs in reverse chronological order. Put the most recent job first and work backward in time.

For each job, write down the following information in this order:

1. Job Title
2. Name of Company or Organization
3. City and State
4. Dates you worked there
5. Responsibilities and Accomplishments

Be sure that you are consistent in the way you write the dates. You don't have to write down the exact day that you started and stopped working at a place. Some possible formats are:

- No months; years only:
  1990-1995

- Months abbreviated:
  Jan 1990-Nov 1995

- Months spelled out:
  January 1990- November 1995

- Months as a number:
  1/1990-11/2000

For your current job, use the word "present" for the "to" date, for example:

1997-present

If you have little or no Work Experience, don't worry. There's a lot more coming up that you can use to show an employer what you can do.

Step 2.2 – Volunteer Experience

Write down the type of same information as for Step 2.1 above.

Step 2.3 – Life Experience

If you are a homemaker or an unskilled worker with a family, you undoubtedly have a lot of Life Experience that is valuable to an employer. For example, as a homemaker or family man, you may have the following Life Experience:

Financial Planner
        Responsible for managing a
        $50,000 per year budget over
        a ten-year period—the financial
        resources of a five-member family

Logistics Supervisor

> Responsible for scheduling and supervising the activities of five individuals over a ten-year period. Planned and implemented transfer of household from New York to California.

Conflict Negotiator

> Responsible for resolving the conflicting needs of five diverse individuals of family unit

Step 2.4 – Personal Qualities

If you consider yourself to be an unskilled worker or if you have little or no Experience, this section gives you a chance to really shine. The information you provide gives the employer a very good idea of what kind of person you are and what it would be like to work with you.

Think of three or four aspects of your personality that you are especially proud of. Then think of a concrete example of something you do that shows each quality in action. For example:

Responsible
> Take care of brothers and sisters in parents' absence

Diligent
> Always put homework before pleasure

Friendly
> Always greet everyone with a smile

Self-starter
> Do household chores without being asked

What you lack in Experience, you can make up for with Personal Qualities. These can help you land your first job.

If you are an unskilled worker with Experience, your Personal Qualities can make you stand out from the crowd and get you hired again and again.

If you are an experienced worker, this information will come in handy when mentioning your Personal Qualities in your cover letter.

Step 2.5 – Education

If you have earned one or more Degrees or Certificates, write them down in reverse order, with the most recent Degree first and the oldest Degree last. For each degree, write down the following information in this order:

1. Degree or Certificate
2. Subject/Department/Specialty
3. Name of Institution or School
4. City and State
5. Year Degree or Certificate was received

A sample entry would be:

BA, Biology
University of Iowa, Iowa City, Iowa
1999

If you did not complete your Degree, write "Undergraduate Studies" or "Graduate Studies" instead of the Degree, and the period of time you studied. For example:

Undergraduate Studies, Biology
University of Illinois
Champagne-Urbana, Illinois
1997-1999

For an uncompleted Certificate or Diploma from a Trade School, write "Professional Studies". For example:

Professional Studies
The Woodworkers Academy
Austin, Texas
1998-1999

If you do not have a college Degree, or you graduated from college very recently, then you should list your high school. For example:

Diploma, 4.0 GPA
Thomas Jefferson High School
St. Louis, Missouri
1989

Only add your Grade Point Average if it was very high.

If you did not graduate from high school, write "Attended" instead of "Graduated". For example:

Attended
Mill Valley High School
Mill Valley, Arkansas
1995-1997

Step 2.6 – Interests & Hobbies

Write down any interests or hobbies that are relevant to the job you are applying for.

If you're applying to work in a flower shop, and you enjoy gardening, write that down.

However, if you like to swim and you're applying for a job reshelving books at a library, don't bother writing about swimming (unless, of course, you're applying to work in a library at a Physical Education school).

Step 2.7 – Languages

If you speak a foreign language, be sure to write this down. Your language skills can be a very valuable asset to any company.

Step 2.8 – Awards/Honors

Write down any awards or honors that show you excel in your field. For example:

Employee of the Year, Costco, Los Angeles, California,1999

Step 2.9 – Professional Skills

Now that you've analyzed your background in depth, it's time to summarize the skills you've developed.

This is very important because, as you'll see, this summary will appear at the top of your résumé.

What do you know? What can you do? Make a list of the skills that are useful for the job you are applying for.

For example, if you are applying for a secretarial position, you might write:

- Fast and accurate typist
- Knowledge of word processing and spreadsheet programs
- Pleasant telephone manner

If you are applying for an entry-level job at a bank, you might write:

- Work well with the public
- Enjoy working with numbers
- Speak fluent Spanish and English

Even if you are an "unskilled worker," you undoubtedly have professional skills that you may be unaware of. For example, you may:

- Have a pleasant telephone manner
- Pack goods in a safe and efficient manner
- Clean rooms thoroughly and quickly
- Speak English and Chinese

Step 3 — Organize Your Notes

Put at the top of your résumé the information most relevant to the job you are applying for. I'll show you how to do this.

Step 3.1 – Name

At the very top of your résumé, write your name.

Step 3.2 – Address, Etc.

Under your name, write your address, phone number, and e-mail address (if you have one).

Step 3.3 – Job Objective

Take a look at Step 1 again. That's where you wrote your Job Objective.

Now, ask yourself, will you accept another kind of job? If the answer is no, then you should put your Job Objective at the top of your résumé, under your name, address and phone number. This way, the employer won't waste your time interviewing you for a job you don't want.

Also ask yourself, is this job a career change for you? If the answer is yes, then you should put your Job Objective at the top of your résumé (under your name, etc.). If you don't, the employer is likely to look at all your experience from your old career and assume that you want more of the same.

Finally, if you have held many different types of jobs in different fields, be sure to include your Job Objective in your résumé. Otherwise, the employer won't be sure what you're interested in doing **now**.

If you are **not** looking for a specific position, and you are interested in being interviewed for a variety of jobs, do not put a Job Objective on your résumé at all but go directly to Professional Skills, instead.

Step 3.4 – Professional Skills

Now add the Professional Skills section that you developed in Step 2.9.

Step 3.5 – Experience

Now you're going to decide what kind of Experience sections to put in your résumé and in which order.

If your Work Experience and Volunteer Experience are in the same field, combine them under one heading called Experience and list each job in reverse chronological order, with the most recent job first.

If your Volunteer Experience relates more to the job you are applying for now than your Work Experience does, put Volunteer Experience *above* Work Experience in your résumé.

If your Volunteer Experience is totally unrelated to the job you are applying for, you can leave it out altogether.

If you do not have any Work Experience or Volunteer Experience, put here your Life Experience, instead.

If you are so young that you do not have any Work Experience, Volunteer Experience or Life Experience, stay tuned for the next step!

Step 3.6 – Personal Qualities

If you are so young that you do not have any Work Experience, Volunteer Experience or Life Experience, this step is for you. Here's the place to put your Personal Qualities, instead.

Also, if you are an unskilled worker with Experience, you can still add here the section on Personal Qualities. This will give an employer even more reasons to hire you.

If you are an experienced worker, do not include in your résumé the section on Personal Qualities. Your well-developed Experience and Professional Skills will speak for themselves. However, keep those adjectives handy because you can use them in your cover letter to mention your Personal Qualities.

Step 3.7 – The Rest

You now have four sections left to consider:

Education
Interests/Hobbies
Languages
Awards/Honors

Among these, the only section that you absolutely must put in is Education. The others are optional.

If your Education directly relates to the job you are applying for, put it in now. If the other sections have more to do with the job you are applying for, put them before Education.

If the other sections have nothing to do with the job you are looking for, leave them out entirely and end your résumé with Education.

Note

You may not have used all the sections you wrote about in Step 2, but don't think for a minute that you wasted your time. There was no other way to learn enough about yourself to write the all-important Professional Skills section.

Step 4 — Edit Your Notes

Use the key words and phrases that tell an employer you are an active and responsible employee.

To help you, we have provided lists of the words and phrases that people commonly use in résumés to write about their Experience, Professional Skills and Personal Qualities.

As you go through the lists and edit your work, keep in mind that you do not have to worry about writing complete sentences. In fact, it is better to use short phrases, without using the word "I", or articles such as "a" and "the". For example:

- Managed team of five salespeople
- Devised efficient order-taking procedures
- Increased annual sales by 15%

Use past tense for previous jobs you have held and present tense for your current job.

Be sure to always spell correctly!
Here, now, are the three lists:

<u>Experience</u>

Use these words to explain what you *did*.

achieved	commissioned	directed
acquired	compiled	distributed
administered	completed	donated
advised	computed	edited
aided	computerized	eliminated
amended	conceived	enabled
analyzed	conducted	enforced
appointed	consolidated	enhanced
approved	contacted	established
arranged	coordinated	estimated
assigned	corresponded	evaluated
assisted	created	examined
attained	customized	exceeded
attended	decreased	executed
audited	defined	extended
authorized	delivered	facilitated
built	demonstrated	forecast
carried out	designed	formulated
chaired	determined	founded
changed	developed	gained
coached	devised	gathered
combined	diagnosed	handled

headed	optimized	reported
held	ordered	researched
helped	organized	resolved
hired	outlined	reviewed
identified	overhauled	revised
implemented	oversaw	routed
improved	participated	scheduled
increased	performed	screened
initiated	persuaded	selected
inspected	planned	served
instituted	prepared	simplified
interviewed	presented	sold
introduced	processed	solicited
invented	programmed	solved
kept	promoted	started
launched	proposed	streamlined
led	proved	studied
maintained	provided	submitted
managed	published	suggested
manufactured	purchased	summarized
marketed	quantified	supervised
maximized	raised	surpassed
negotiated	recommended	surveyed
notified	recruited	taught
obtained	rectified	tested
offered	referred	tracked
operated	refined	traded

trained	upgraded	won
troubleshot	used	worked out
uncovered	utilized	wrote
updated	volunteered	yielded

Professional Skills

Use these phrases to explain what you **know** and what you can do well.

accomplished in
computer literate
experience in/with
excellent written and verbal
    communication
experienced in/with
good interpersonal skills
expert in
expertise in
facility with
familiar with
fluent in
knowledge of
knowledgeable about
practiced in
proficient in/with
seasoned in
skilled in/with

Personal Qualities

Use these words and phrases to describe what you are like.

able to multi-task
able to work independently
articulate
caring
compassionate
dependable
detail-oriented
enthusiastic
follow instructions well
friendly
hard-working
industrious
motivated
polite
resourceful
results-oriented
self-starter
take direction well
team player

Step 5 — Type Your Résumé

Lay out the information neatly and in such a manner that the important information stands out.

If you do not want to type the résumé yourself, go to a professional typist. Do not give an employer a hand-written résumé.

I will help you take the guesswork out of which résumé style to use by showing you exactly what to do to achieve out-standing professional results. See the following pages for sample résumés.

CHARLES SIMMONS

1903 Maple Drive
Anytown, Michigan 48105
Tel.: (734) 555-1275
E-mail: cxsimmons@eandegroup.com

PROFESSIONAL SKILLS

- Providing psychological and behavioral counseling to disturbed pets and their owners

- Writing newspaper columns on the care of pets and the plight of endangered species in the wild

- Performing in public with trained and wild animals

WORK EXPERIENCE

Pet Psychologist

Private Practice, Ann Arbor, Michigan
1995-present

Founded and maintain private practice which serves over 1000 new clients every year

Entertainer

The Tonight Show, Burbank, California
1995-present

Make regular television appearances to showcase unusual animals and to increase awareness of endangered species

Newspaper Columnist

Morgan Newspaper Group,
Chicago, Illinois
1993-present

Write syndicated column on animal life that appears in over 400 newspapers across the country

EDUCATION

Doctor of Veterinary Medicine

School of Veterinary Medicine
University of Michigan
Ann Arbor, Michigan
1990

Bachelor of Science

Zoology
University of Nebraska
Omaha, Nebraska
1985

MARIE PHILLIPS

1001 Warren Street
Anytown, Illinois 60201
Tel.: (847) 555-3359

PROFESSIONAL SKILLS

- Analyzing and designing the functional requirements of large-scale software systems

- Designing the user interface of software programs

- Writing and designing on-line and print user manuals and other technical documentation

- Designing and programming Web sites

WORK EXPERIENCE

Interface Designer
Head Technical Writer
Web Master

Libraries Unlimited, Chicago, Illinois
March 1997-October 1999

- Designed the user interface of Web-based modules of *FORWARD*, a leading computerized library management system.

- Wrote and designed on-line and print user manuals and other technical documentation.

- Designed and wrote interactive Web-Based user manuals and Windows-based user manuals and on-line help.

- Designed and maintained Company Web site.

- Trained and supervised technical writers.

System Designer
Writer

Supermedia, Chicago, Illinois
February 1995-January 1997

- Wrote the functional specifications and designed the user interface of a computerized system for tracking all forms of media (including 50,000 images and 800 hours of video and animation) developed by the Company for use worldwide

- Wrote award-winning multimedia edutainment CDs for the American consumer market.

System Designer
Technical Writer

Eduworld Ltd., Los Angeles, California
May 1987-January 1990

- Designed the *Fun with Science* class management system. This was Eduworlds' flagship product, used by more than 400,000 students worldwide.

- Wrote the functional specifications, designed the user interface and wrote the on-line help and user manual for an instructional management system designed for IBM by a team of 25 software designers and programmers.

- Developed educational software for a joint venture with Prentice Hall. Curriculum areas included physics, chemistry, biology and earth science.

EDUCATION

Doctoral Studies

Visual Scholars Program
University of Iowa, Iowa City, Iowa
January 1978-March 1981

An interdisciplinary PhD program studying visual learning, thinking and communicating. Studies included cognitive psychology, film & broadcasting, and instructional design.

Master of Arts

Library and Information Science
University of Iowa
August 1980

Reference services
Computer-assisted information storage & retrieval

Bachelor of Arts

Biology, University of Iowa
December 1976

Step 5.1 – Choose Your Paper

Use an 8½ x 11 sheet of paper. The weight of the paper should be what is called 20 lb. (lb.=pound) or 24 lb. paper. Use white, cream or light gray.

Step 5.2 – Choose Your Typeface

The typeface is also called the "font". Use either Arial or Times New Roman.

This is an example of Arial.

This is an example of Times New Roman.

Do not mix fonts in the same résumé. Use *either* Arial *or* Times New Roman.

I will show you when to use **bold**, *italics*, CAPS, and <u>underlined</u> text.

Step 5.3 – Choose Your Font Sizes

Now for font sizes. (Font sizes are defined by "points".)

If you choose Arial, you will use two font sizes, 12 point and 10 point.

This is an example of 12 point Arial.

This is an example of 10 point Arial.

If you choose Times New Roman, you will use these two font sizes: 14 point and 12 point.

This is an example of 14 point Times New Roman.

This is an example of 12 point Times New Roman.

Step 5.4 – Type Your Résumé

Now you are ready to start typing your résumé.

Step 5.4.1 – Your Name

Type your **NAME** in **BOLD CAPITAL LETTERS** at the top of the page. If you are using Arial, type in 12 point. If you are using Times New Roman, type in 14 point. Center your name in the middle of the line.

Under your name, type a line going across the page, as follows:

NAME

_____

Step 5.4.2 – Your Address, etc.

Under the line you drew, type your street address, city, state, phone number and e-mail address (if you have one) in regular letters (not bold). If you are using

Arial, type in 10 point. If you are using Times New Roman, type in 12 point. Center the information the way you did for your name:

NAME

_____

Street
City, State, Zip
Telephone Number

Step 5.4.3 – Job Objective

Drop down three lines and type ***JOB OBJECTIVE*** as follows:

JOB OBJECTIVE   President of airline
                                  company

Type the ***JOB OBJECTIVE*** heading in ***BOLD UNDERLINED CAPITALIZED ITALICS***, starting at the left margin. Use Arial 10 point or Times New Roman 12 point.

To type the Description, indent and type in regular letters. Use Arial 10 point or Times New Roman 12 point.

Step 5.4.4 – Professional Skills

Drop down another two or three lines and type ***PROFESSIONAL SKILLS*** as follows:

PROFESSIONAL SKILLS

- Description of your first skill or area of expertise

- Description of your second skill or area of expertise

Type the ***PROFESSIONAL SKILLS*** heading in ***BOLD UNDERLINED CAPITALIZED ITALICS***, starting at the left margin. Use Arial 10 point or Times New Roman 12 point.

To type the Descriptions of your skills, indent and type in regular letters. Use Arial 10 point or Times New Roman 12 point. Use bullets for your list of descriptions, as shown above. If your Descriptions run more than one line, indent all the lines and make sure that they all start at the same column.

Step 5.4.5 – Experience

The following format is for any kind of Experience section that you are including in your résumé, be it Experience, Work Experience, Volunteer Experience or Life Experience:

WORK EXPERIENCE

Job Title   **Company/Organization Name
City, State**
"From" Date-"To" Date

                    • Description of accomplishments and responsibilities

                    • Description of accomplishments and responsibilities in a second area

Type the section heading (in the above example it is **_WORK EXPERI-_**

ENCE), in ***BOLD UNDERLINED CAPI-TALIZED ITALICS***. Use Arial 10 point or Times New Roman 12 point.

Type the **Job Title** and **Company/Organization Name** in **Upper- and Lowercase Bold Letters.** Use Arial 10 point or Times New Roman 12 point. If you are including a Life Experience section, you would, of course, omit the Company/Organization Name.

If the Job Title is very long, break it up and put it on more than one line, like this:

WORK EXPERIENCE

Manager of	**Company/Organization Name**
Human Resources	**City, State**
	"From" Date-"To" Date
	• Description of accomplish-ments and responsibilities
	• Description of accomplish-ments and responsibilities in a second area

For City, State, Dates and Descriptions, indent and type in regular letters, 10 point Arial or 12 point Times New Roman.

For dates, use ***one*** of the following formats:

- No months; years only:
  1990-1995

- Months abbreviated:
  Jan 1990-Nov 1995

- Months spelled out:
  January 1990- November 1995

- Months as a number:
  1/1990-11/2000

It doesn't matter which one you use, just be consistent and use the same format everywhere.

Use bullets for your list of Descriptions, as shown above. If your Descriptions run more than one line, indent all the lines and make sure that they all start at the same column.

Note

Leave two or three blank lines between each job that you are writing about.
(See sample résumés in this manual.)

Step 5.4.6 – Personal Qualities

If you are including a Personal Qualities section, follow this format:

PERSONAL QUALITIES

Responsible   Description of behavior that
                         Illustrates this quality

Diligent   Description of behavior that
                         Illustrates this quality

Type the heading ***PERSONAL
QUALITIES*** in ***BOLD UNDERLINED
CAPITALIZED ITALICS.*** Use Arial 10
point or Times New Roman 12 point.

Type the **Quality** in **Upper- and
Lowercase Bold Letters.** Use Arial 10
point or Times New Roman 12 point.

Indent the Descriptions and type them in regular letters, using Arial 10 point or Times New Roman 12 point. If your Descriptions run more than one line, indent all the lines and make sure that they all start at the same column. Do not use bullets since you should have only one Description per Personal Quality.

Step 5.4.7 – The Rest

Depending on what you decided in Step 3.7, you now have one or more of the following sections left to type:

Education
Interests/Hobbies
Languages
Awards/Honors

Follow the order you decided upon in Step 3.7, but use the following formats when you type:

EDUCATION

Degree   **Subject**
                              Institution
                              City, State
                              Date

Type **_EDUCATION_** in **_BOLD UN-DERLINED CAPITALIZED ITALICS._** Use Arial 10 point or Times New Roman 12 point.

Type the **Degree** and **Subject** in **Upper- and Lowercase Bold Letters.** Use Arial 10 point or Times New Roman 12 point.

Type the Institution, City, State and Date in normal letters, Arial 10 point or Times New Roman 12 point.

INTERESTS/HOBBIES   Skiing, windsurfing, sailing

Type **_INTERESTS/HOBBIES_** in **_BOLD UNDERLINED CAPITALIZED ITALICS._** Use Arial 10 point or Times New Roman 12 point.

Indent the list of Interests/Hobbies and type in regular letters, Arial 10 point or Times New Roman 12 point. Use commas between each Interest; do not make a bulleted list.

LANGUAGES	Fluent English, German; able to read and write Spanish and French

Type ***LANGUAGES*** in ***BOLD UNDERLINED CAPITALIZED ITALICS.*** Use Arial 10 point or Times New Roman 12 point.

Indent the Description and type in regular letters, Arial 10 point or Times New Roman 12 point. Use semi-colons between each phrase; do not make a bulleted list.

AWARDS/HONORS

Name of Award	**Company/Organization Name** City, State Date(s)
Name of Honor	**Company/Organization Name** City, State Date(s)

Type ***<u>AWARDS/HONORS</u>*** in ***<u>BOLD UNDERLINED CAPITALIZED ITAL-ICS</u>***. Use Arial 10 point or Times New Roman 12 point.

Type the **Name of the Award/ Honor** and **Company/Institution Name** in **Upper- and Lowercase Bold Letters.** Use Arial 10 point or Times New Roman 12 point. If the Job title is very long, break it up and put it on more than one line.

For City, State and Date(s), indent and type in regular letters, 10 point Arial or 12 point Times New Roman.

Step 5.4.8 – Footer and Header

If your résumé is more than one page, add a Footer to the bottom of each page with the page number, for example:

Page 1 of 2

At the top of the second page, type this:

NAME
Continued

Type your **NAME** in the center of the line (as you did on the first page). Under your **NAME**, instead of typing your address and other particulars, type **Continued**. Then type a line across the page and drop down two to three lines before continuing to type the rest of your résumé.

Summary of Step 5

If you have followed the above steps, you have created a very scannable résumé from which it is easy for any employer to see the main points.

A brief glance down the left-hand column shows, for example, your Job Titles and Degrees. These are, after all, the main points.

Unfortunately, many people make the mistake of emphasizing the **dates** by putting **them** in the left-hand column. This is a mistake because most employers care more about **what** you did than **when** you did it.

This point is just one of the many considerations that went into the design of the résumé format that you have learned here.

You can be sure that by following the above instructions, your résumé will be a winner!

Step 6 — Write Your Cover Letter

You should always send a cover letter with your résumé. I have provided two sample cover letters for you to study. When you write your cover letter, be sure to do the following:

1. Type your name, address and phone number at the top of the page, just like you did in your résumé.

2. Type the date.

3. Type the name, Job Title and address of the person to whom you are sending your résumé.

4. For the salutation, write the person's name, for example:

Dear Ms. Applegate,

If you do not know the name of the person to whom you are writing, type:

Dear Sirs:

5. Tell the reader why you are writing. (See the sample cover letters.) If you are applying for a specific job, write the Job Title. If you saw the job advertised, write where you saw the ad.

6. Summarize your experience and qualifications.

7. Refer the reader to your résumé.

8. Tell the reader you look forward to hearing from him/her.

9. Thank the reader for his/her consideration.

10. Close the letter. If you know the reader's name, close with:

Yours sincerely,

If you do ***not*** know the reader's name, close with:

Very truly yours,

Then leave four blank lines and type your name. Sign your name in ink above where you typed it.

On the following pages you will find the sample cover letters.

JANNA JONES

938 Summit Drive
Anytown, Illinois 60201
Tel.: (847) 555-3359

March 7, 2003

Mr. Fred Peabody
Chairman of the Board
Green Acres Hospice
1732 Green Acres Road
Cedar Rapids, Iowa 52402

Dear Mr. Peabody,

I am writing to apply for the position of Hospice Director that I saw advertised in the Des Moines Register.

As a dedicated health professional, I have over 17 years' experience in the Health Care field. For the past five years, I have served as Head of the Nursing Staff of the Oncology Department at the University of Iowa.

I believe in the importance of providing compassionate Health Care and a dignified quality of life to all who suffer from a terminal illness.

For more information on my background, please see the enclosed resume.

Thank you for your consideration. I look forward to hearing from you soon.

Yours sincerely,

Janna Jones, R.N.

WALTER BAINES

2324 Butterfield Road
Anytown, Mississippi 39211
Tel.: (601) 555-3357

January 10, 2003

Human Resources Department
Home Depot
1001 Redwood Drive
Jackson, Mississippi 39211

Dear Sirs:

I am writing to apply for a position with your company.

I am familiar with a wide range of hardware and household tools and their uses.

In High School, I excelled in Shop classes and in my spare time I built a sled, bookcase and a radio.

I am a hard worker and enjoy helping people. I would appreciate the opportunity to start my career with your company.

For more information, please see the enclosed resume.

Thank you for your consideration. I look forward to hearing from you soon.

Very truly yours,

Walter Baines

Afterword

If you have followed all the steps in this manual, you now have a résumé that you can be proud of. You can be sure that it will help you get that job!

Good luck!

About the Author

Stephen Summerford, MLS, learned the secrets of writing successful resumes through his long association with *Personnel Associates, Inc.,* a national consulting firm.

Mr. Summerford is a professional writer who specializes in how-to manuals and educational software. He is an expert at making complex subjects easy to understand.

With your career on the line, don't take chances—learn from the best!

Printed in the United States
25257LVS00001B/247